THIS HALLOWEEN ACTIVITY BOOK BELONGS TO:

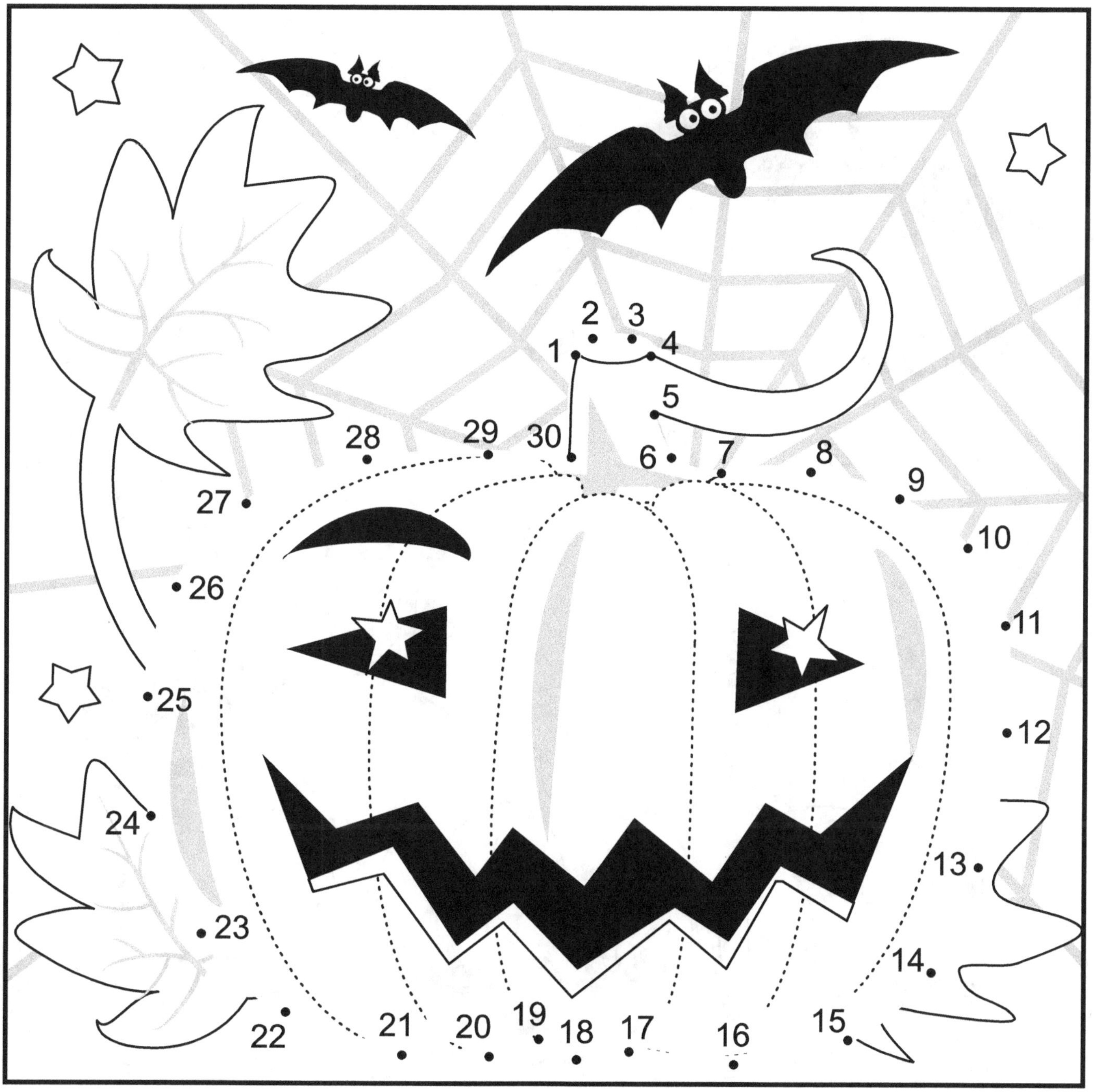

TIPS AND TRICKS FOR USING THIS ACTIVITY BOOK:

THIS BOOK HAS BEEN DESIGNED FOR YOUNG CHILDREN TO ENJOY HALLOWEEN WITH THESE FUN ACTIVITIES: COUNTING, COMPARING, PROBLEM SOLVING, DRAWING, COLORING & CUTTING, MATH, AND THINKING SKILLS! THE ANSWERS ARE FOUND ON PAGES 46-47 FOR YOUR CONVENIENCE. THE COLOR, CUT, & GLUE PAGES HAVE BEEN PLACED ON ONE SIDE, SO THEY CAN BE EASILY BE REMOVED.

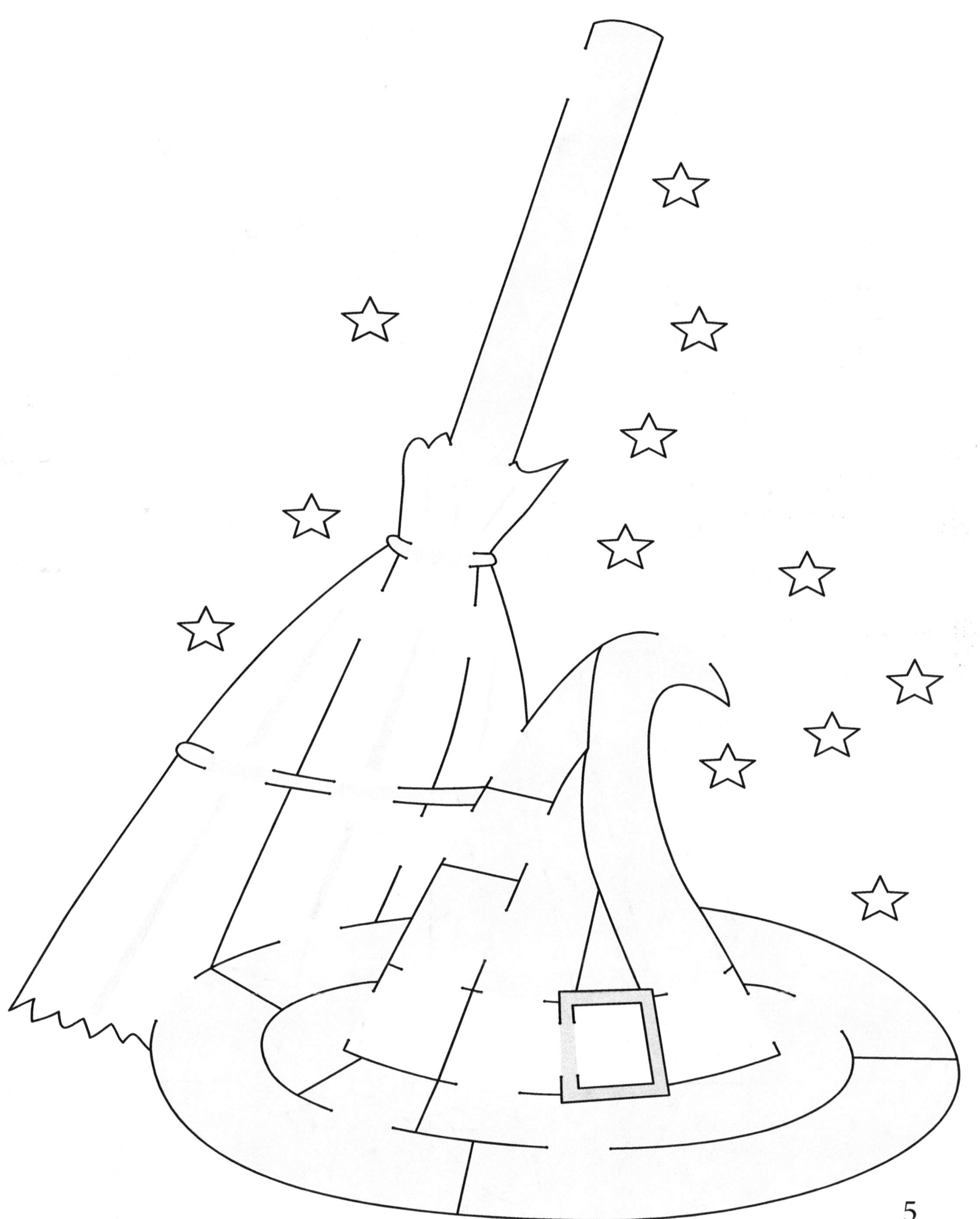

5

HOW MANY?

HOW MANY?

COUNT
&
CALCULATE

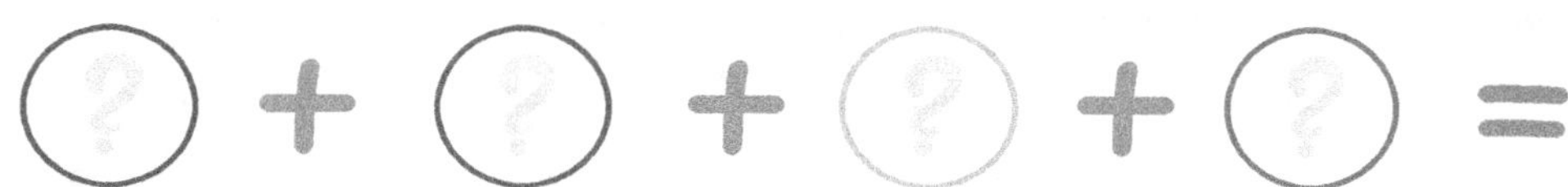

0 + 0 + 0 + 0 = 0

0 1 2 3 4 5 6 7 8 9 + −
10 11 12 13 14 15 16 17 18 19 20 =

0 1 2 3 4 5 6 7 8 9

HOW
MANY
FRUITS
DO YOU SEE?
?

FIND
ONE
PICTURE
WITHOUT A COPY

1	g				e
2	w				n
3	m				y
4	d				s
5	t				s
6	p				a
7	c				r
8	a				w
9	p				a
10	d				t

and   oma   onu   aco   umm

res   hai   rro   izz   lov

z _ _ _ _ e   p _ _ _ _ i n
s _ _ _ _ r   v _ _ _ _ r e
c _ _ _ e   c _ _ _ k e
ampi   ombi
astl   upca
pide   umpk

1.

◯ − ◯ = ◯

2.

◯ − ◯ = ◯

3.

◯ − ◯ = ◯

0 1 2 3 4 5 6 7 8 9 + −
10 11 12 13 14 15 16 17 18 19 20 =

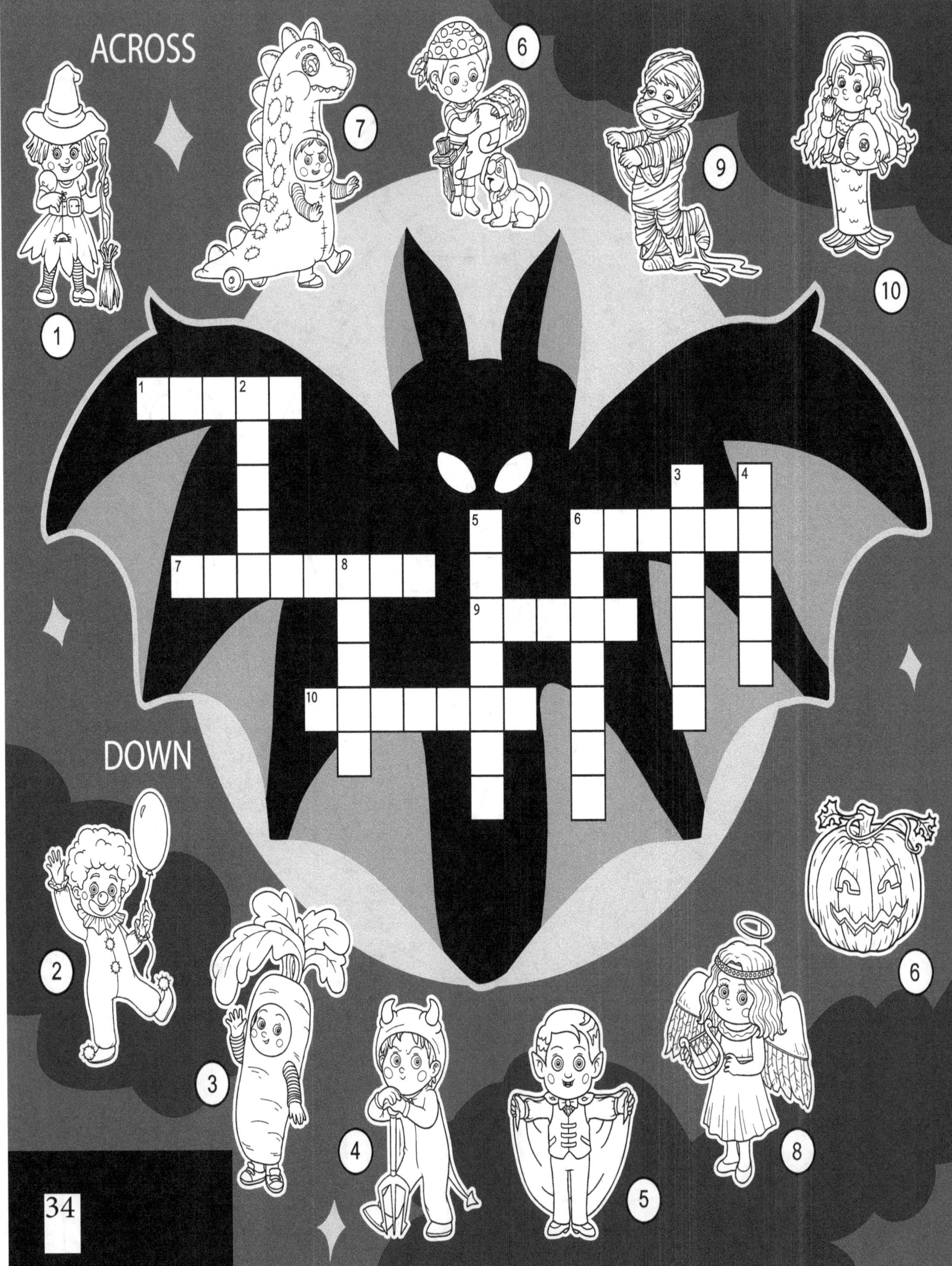
ACROSS
DOWN
34

OCTOBER

CUT & GLUE
COLOR
1
CUT OUT
2
GLUE
3
USE EXAMPLE OR YOUR IMAGINATION

CUT & GLUE
COLOR
1
CUT OUT
2
GLUE
3
USE EXAMPLE OR YOUR IMAGINATION

CUT & GLUE
COLOR
1
CUT OUT
2
GLUE
3
USE EXAMPLE OR YOUR IMAGINATION

CUT & GLUE
COLOR
1
CUT OUT
2
GLUE
3
USE EXAMPLE OR YOUR IMAGINATION
43

HALLOWEEN

ANSWER KEY:

Page 1

Page 2

Page 3

Page 4

Page 5

Page 6

Page 7

Page 8

Page 14

$5 + 7 + 3 + 1 = 16$
(any combination of
these numbers to = 16)

Page 9

Page 10

Page 11

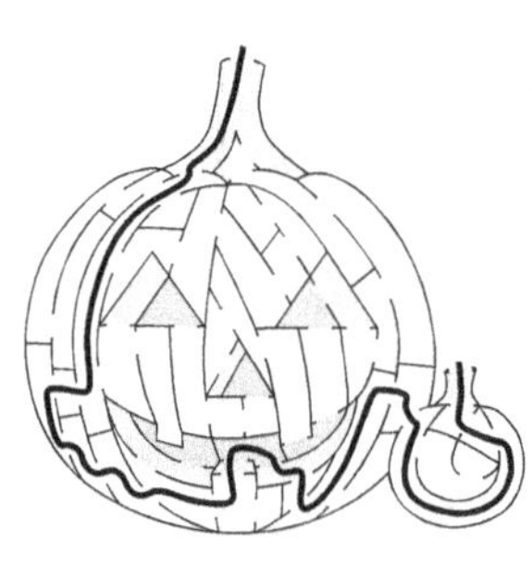

Page 12

7

9

6

5

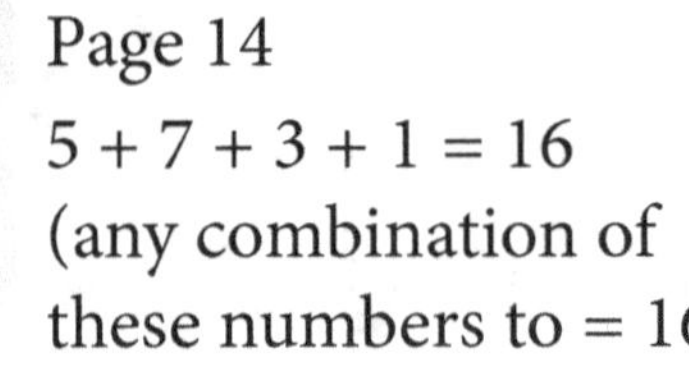

Page 14

$1 + 3 + 4 + 2 = 10$
(any combination of
these numbers to =10)

Page 15

$1 + 2 + 3 + 6 = 12$
(any combination of
these numbers to =12)

Page 16

17 fruits

Page 17

cucumber

Page 18

skull
mummy
witch
ghost
candy
devil

Page 19

hat
bat
cat
eye
web

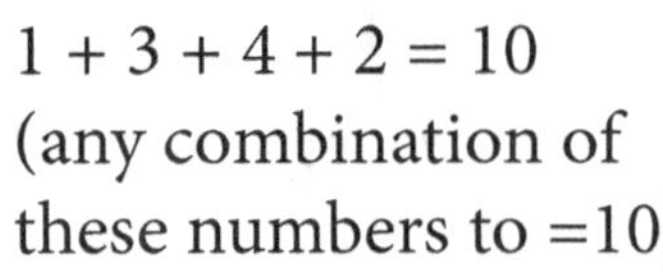

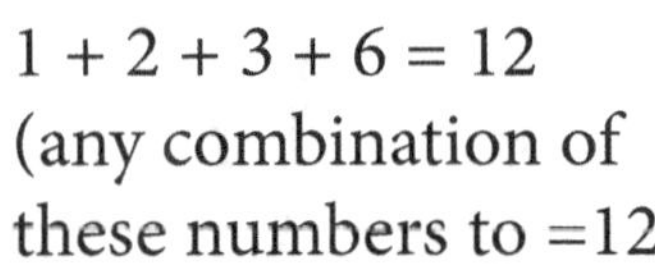

Page 20
glove
woman
mummy
dress
tacos
pizza or panda
chair
arrow
panda or pizza
donut

Page 21
zombie
spider
castle
pumpkin
vampire
cupcake

Page 22
Matching
eggs-bunny
pumpkin-witch
couple-cupid
gifts-Santa

Page 23
6 - 1 = 5

Page 24-25
answer key not
available

Page 26-31
Draw and color these
Halloween images.

Page 32

Page 33

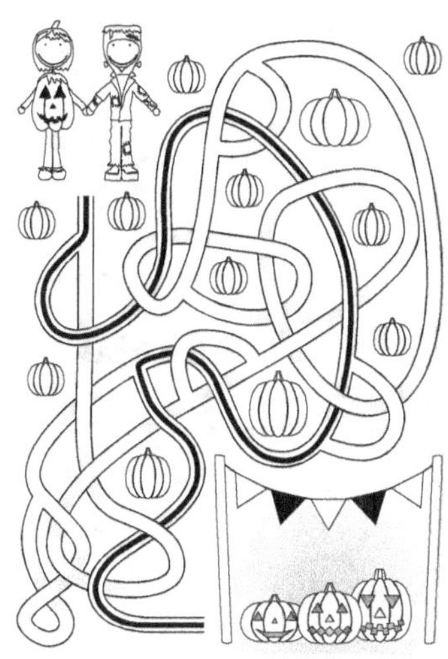

Page 34
across:
1. witch
6. pirate
7. dinosaur
9. mummy
10.mermaid
down:
2. clown
3. carrot
4. devil
5. vampire
6. pumpkin
8. angel

Page 35
Use your favorite colors!

Pages 37-43
Color, cut, & glue these
on another sheet of
paper.

Pages 45
Use your favorite colors!

THANK YOU FOR YOUR RECENT PURCHASE. WE HOPE YOU'VE BEEN ENJOYING THIS HALLOWEEN ACTIVITY BOOK. PLEASE VISIT OUR WEBSITE FOR NEWS ABOUT FUTURE BOOKS AND SUGGESTED FRIENDLY READS FOR CHILDREN AND ADULTS BY CAREFULLY SELECTED AUTHORS. IF YOU WOULD LIKE US TO PUBLISH A BOOK ON A SPECIFIC TOPIC, LET US KNOW. WE WELCOME YOUR IDEAS!

florabella.com

florabellapublishing@yahoo.com

florabellapublsihing, LLC